D0364427

DAISY LOWE

SWEETNESS

Quadrille
PUBLISHING

&LIGHT

Portrait photography by Guy Aroch | Food photography by Ali Allen

contents

INTRODUCTION

My sugar addiction began at an early age. My Gramps used to take me to school and give me money for the sweet shop. I would buy bags of penny sweets and eat them all. It was the start of a life-long love affair and I still have the world's biggest sweet tooth.

These days, I am a model so I have to look after my body. More importantly, there are huge health implications to living on sugar. I had to find other ways to get my sweet fix.

I never thought it would be possible for me to kick the sugar habit until I moved to New York. There, I tasted natural products that give you a sweet hit without harming your body. Recently I also found out that I am intolerant to wheat and dairy. A few of the healthy substitutions I've made for wheat, dairy and sugar in these recipes will be new to you, but you will easily be able to find them in health food shops and online. My body feels so much healthier and it works better. I have more energy, I sleep better, I get sick less often. I am feeding myself, not starving or depriving myself of the sweet things I love. I wanted to share these recipes so you can do the same, and love yourself from the inside out.

I have always loved baking and some of my fondest early memories are of cooking with mum. Growing up, a birthday gift to friends was always different variations on vanilla sponge. So when I found out I was intolerant to wheat, I started looking for recipes that were largely gluten-free but still delicious.

I have inspired some friends to eat better and exercise more, and that was another reason to write this book, to reach a wider audience. More people are thinking about what they put into their bodies and how they look after them. I work out three times a week, I love Pilates and going to the gym and I meditate. Exercise makes my brain sharper and helps me feel so much brighter. The release of endorphins and getting your body going are really important.

It's taken me a long time to appreciate my curves but the female form is so beautiful – as women we deserve to feel more comfortable in it. I want women to stop feel guilty about food and to feel better from within. Life is short and we need to enjoy every moment. Love yourself. Eat well. Life is sweet!

Heart code

 GLUTEN-FREE

 DAIRY-FREE

 VEGAN

 REFINED SUGAR-FREE

Gluten-free Goodies

Brown rice flakes
These are wonderfully creamy when mixed with liquid, but also crunchy when toasted. They are digested slowly so you feel full for longer.

Buckwheat flour
First farmed 6,000 years ago, this highly nutritious grain has a wonderfully nutty taste.

Millet flour
Golden and subtly sweet, this is a great flour to use in gluten-free baked goods.

Quinoa, or quinoa flakes, or pops or puffs
A seed rather than a grain, quinoa in its many forms is a complete protein, containing all eight of the essential amino acids our bodies need.

And a final gluten-free note...
If a recipe calls for baking powder, use gluten-free baking powder, or all your good gluten-free work will be undone! And make sure your bags of goodies are *labelled* gluten-free, too, as others may have been processed with gluten.

U is for Unicorn

Refined sugar-free goodies

♥ ♥ ♥ ♥

Organic agave syrup
Sweeter than honey and made from the same plant used to make tequila! This has a lower GI than most other natural sweeteners. Look for bottles labelled 'organic', to avoid imposters.

Organic maple syrup
An excellent source of manganese, which promotes energy and is an antioxidant, as well as zinc, which helps maintain a healthy immune system… but mostly, just yummy. Again, an organic bottle is a safe bet.

Palm sugar (and coconut palm sugar)
Nutrient-rich and completely natural, with a richer taste than refined sugar, this won't cause blood sugar spikes.

Raw honey
This has not been heat-treated or processed, so all the magical flower-based nutrients are still there.

Dairy-free goodies

♥ ♥ ♥ ♥

Milk
It's really not hard to live without dairy, and many people are intolerant to the lactose (milk sugar) in dairy products. Instead, try one of the plant-based milks – almond, soya, rice, oat or hemp – which are widely available.

Butter
In baking, cacao butter and coconut butter are both useful, natural substitutes for regular butter.

Cream
Oat cream can replace regular cream in a baking recipe when only small amounts are needed.

Yogurt
Anyone who has tried soya yogurt or coconut yogurt doesn't need to be convinced: wonderfully creamy-tasting and healthy, too.

secret ingredients

Avocados
Protein, good fats, anti-inflammatory, and unique in the plant world in giving desserts a creamy mouth feel without the use of other fats or any dairy.

Bananas
Packed with potassium, which is great for heart function, they are also claimed to promote relaxation and a feeling of well-being.

Bee pollen
Granules of nutritious pollen made by bees with added honey or nectar, packed with vitamins and minerals and oh, so sweet.

Cacao powder
Pretty much the same as cocoa powder, but likely to be far less processed.

Chia seeds
High in minerals and healthy omega-3 fats, these prevent blood sugar spikes and give you fibre, too. They are rich in calcium as well, so are good for your teeth and bones.

Coconut oil
An easily digested natural fat that is also highly nutritious.

Goji berries
Beautiful to look at and long used in Chinese medicine to manage diabetes and high blood pressure. These are antioxidant and may also boost the immune system.

Maca powder
This powdered root is thought to protect against stress, balance hormones and increase metabolism.

Mesquite powder
A ground-up bean pod, this is high in protein and a good source of soluble fibre; it digests slowly and does not cause spikes in blood sugar.

Xylitol
A sweetener made from xylan, which is found in plant fibres, this has a gentler effect on your blood sugar than regular sugar. It's also claimed to be good for your teeth!

BreakFast

GOODY-GOODIES

This is my favourite granola as there are so many great things about it! It's super-tasty, nutty, crunchy and full of all the things that are good for you: protein from nuts; omega-3, minerals and fibre from seeds; and vitamins and antioxidants from berries.

RISE& SHINE GraNOLa

♥ ♥ ♥ ♥

2 tbsp coconut oil, plus more if needed
200g mixed nuts, such as almonds, hazelnuts, walnuts and Brazil nuts
50g quinoa flakes
50g brown rice flakes
50g gluten-free oats
50g quinoa pops or puffs
50g mixed seeds, such as flax seeds, chia seeds, pumpkin seeds and sunflower seeds
100g dates, chopped
20g organic cacao powder (optional)
4 tbsp organic agave syrup, plus more if needed
50g coconut flakes
30g dried strawberries, chopped
50g dried cranberries

Makes 700–800g

Preheat the oven to 160°C/gas mark 3. Gently melt the coconut oil in a small saucepan over a medium heat, being careful not to let it get too hot. Remove from the heat and brush half of it over a large, deep baking tray.

Place all the nuts in a large mixing bowl and lightly crush them with a pestle or the end of a rolling pin. Add the quinoa flakes, brown rice flakes, oats, quinoa pops, seeds and dates and mix it all together. Stir in the cacao powder, if using. Stir in the remaining coconut oil until everything is evenly coated.

Add the agave syrup and give it a stir, making sure the whole mixture looks moist. If you think it seems a bit dry, add a little more melted coconut oil or agave syrup. Some of the granola will clump together, but that just adds to the texture.

Tip the mixture into the prepared baking tray and spread it level. Place in the oven for eight to 10 minutes, keeping an eye on it and stirring it every couple of minutes, as it is quick to burn.

Once it looks toasted and golden, remove the tray from the oven and leave to cool. Add the coconut and dried berries.

When cold, store the granola in an airtight container. Enjoy it sprinkled over porridge, as a breakfast cereal with almond milk or soya yogurt, or simply as a crunchy afternoon snack.

When I was recently in Greece on holiday, I took some rye bread with me. I was used to having peanut butter or avocado and chilli flakes piled on the rye toast, but one morning I fancied something sweet. Since I was in Greece, I thought I would make the most of their amazing honey. I couldn't believe how delicious this was; it tasted like a banoffee pie yet was made from just three good-for-you ingredients. This is a complete winner. Rye bread fills you up for longer than wheat and lowers the insulin response, too.

BaNaNa& HoNeYon rYeToast

2 slices of rye bread

1 ripe banana

2 tsp raw honey

Serves 1

Toast the bread until golden on both sides. Meanwhile, peel and thinly slice the banana. Lightly mash it with a fork, if you want.

Once the bread is toasted, top each slice with the banana and drizzle with the honey. Eat straight away.

Do you like jelly? Chocolate? If you answer 'yes' to both questions, then you should love this. Chia seeds have become extremely popular recently and it is claimed they will make you feel fuller both faster and for longer. They also contain brilliant things such as calcium, magnesium and phosphorous and are generally so good for you that I had to figure out a way of including them in this book.

CHOCOLATE, COCONUT & CHIASEED WAKE-UP CALL

♥ ♥ ♥ ♥

150g chia seeds
550ml coconut water
2 tbsp coconut oil
2 tbsp organic cacao powder
2 tbsp coconut cream
1 tbsp organic maple syrup
mixed berries, to serve
soya yogurt, to serve

Serves 4–6

Place the chia seeds and coconut water in a mixing bowl. Leave to soak for 35–45 minutes, stirring occasionally.

In a small pan over a medium heat, lightly melt the coconut oil just until it becomes liquid. Add it to the chia seeds with the cacao powder, coconut cream and maple syrup and stir well.

Serve with some berries and a dollop of soya yogurt.

If I fancy a change from Rise & shine granola (see page 14), I will make a batch of muesli on a Sunday for the week ahead. I ate muesli for breakfast when I was growing up, and I remember the joy of finding sweet little gems of raisins and sultanas throughout. When I began avoiding refined sugar and wheat, I had to give up store-bought muesli, so it was vital to find a way of making my own!

HEALTHY BREAKFAST MUESLI

150g gluten-free oats

150g mixed whole nuts, such as pecans, walnuts, hazelnuts and pine nuts

60g mixed seeds, such as pumpkin seeds and sunflower seeds

60g flaked almonds

2 tbsp palm sugar

½ tsp sea salt

100g dried fruit, such as apricots, sultanas and dates

Serves 4

Place the oats in a large dry frying pan over a medium heat. Toast gently for five minutes, shaking the pan occasionally to prevent them burning. Transfer to a large bowl to cool.

Tip the nuts (except the almonds) into the same pan and again toast gently until golden, around five minutes. Pour them into the bowl of oats. Add the seeds and almonds to the pan and toast for another three minutes until golden, shaking occasionally to prevent them burning. Pour these, too, into the bowl of oats.

Add the palm sugar and salt to the pan and heat for another two minutes, breaking up any lumps. Add the dried fruit and stir together. Once again, tip the contents of the pan into the bowl of oats and mix well. Allow to cool completely.

When cold, store the muesli in an airtight container.

cacao smoothie

♥ ♥ ♥ ♥

This is one of my absolute favourite things! I love it. The recipe was inspired by a drink I had at one of the best smoothie bars in LA: Earthbar. I tried to recreate it as soon as I got back to London and this is the closest I could get. This gives me sustained energy, makes me feel happy and even seems to make my brain work better.

2 tbsp organic cacao powder
1 tbsp maca powder
1 tbsp mesquite powder (optional)
500ml hemp milk
6 tbsp organic agave syrup
handful of ice cubes

Serves 4–6

Place everything in a food processor and blitz until completely combined.

Voila! Ready to drink.

Banana smoothie

♥ ♥

If I am in a rush and have only got a few minutes before leaving the house, I will quickly whizz this up. It is the perfect morning recipe to have up your sleeve when you have been unable to organize your week. Blitz it, pop it in a cup or bottle and drink it on your way to work.

3 ripe bananas
1 tbsp coconut oil
300ml almond milk
200g organic Greek or
    soya yogurt
$\frac{1}{2}$ tbsp ground cinnamon, plus
    more to serve (optional)
2 tbsp raw honey
handful of ice cubes

Serves 4–6

Peel and roughly chop the bananas. Place all the ingredients in a food processor and blitz until smooth and creamy.

Serve immediately, sprinkled with a little cinnamon, if you want.

LOVE YOURSELF FROM

THE INSIDE OUT

I came up with this recipe while cooking with my mum. It is a naturally sweet porridge that offers sustainable energy throughout the morning. This is especially good to eat before a gym session because it gives you a slow release of energy as you work out.

QUINOA& BANANA PORRIDGE

1 tbsp coconut oil

3 ripe bananas

finely grated zest and juice of
   1 organic or unwaxed lime,
   plus more to serve (optional)

200g cooked Quinoa
   (see page 133)

couple of pinches of ground
   cinnamon, to serve

berries, to serve (optional)

Serves 4

Gently melt the coconut oil in a small saucepan over a medium heat until just liquid.

Peel and cut the bananas into chunks. In a mixing bowl, mash the bananas with a fork and add the coconut oil, lime zest and juice. Stir together until well mixed, then gently stir in the cooled quinoa until just combined.

Serve in bowls, sprinkled with a little cinnamon, adding more lime zest or a handful of berries, if you like.

This is the breakfast I have when I am going to be on an underwear shoot, or on the beach. It is the lightest breakfast you can eat, but it still gives me the much-needed injection of sweetness that I crave to keep me going.

apple salad with star anise syrup

♥ ♥ ♥ ♥

4 tbsp palm sugar
2 cinnamon sticks
2 star anise
4 crisp apples, such as
   Granny Smith
juice of $\frac{1}{2}$ a lemon

Serves 4

Put the palm sugar, cinnamon and star anise in a saucepan. Pour in 100ml of water, place over a high heat and bring to the boil. Boil rapidly for 15 minutes until the liquid has reduced and has a syrup-like consistency.

Leaving the apples whole, slice them into thin rounds, starting from one end and working your way down. The pips will fall out as you slice and you will get a lovely star shape in the middle. Squeeze over the lemon juice to avoid the apples browning.

Divide the apple slices between four plates and drizzle over the spiced syrup to serve.

I am a huge fan of the breakfast pancake, especially the American 'stack' variety. I am *so* proud of this recipe! I spent a really long time trying to perfect them, as I was hell-bent on getting mine to taste and look as good as the typical American pancakes. These are easy to digest and won't hurt your stomach if you have a wheat intolerance. Surprisingly, they are wonderfully nutritious and will sustain your energy levels.

BUCKWHEAT PANCAKES

♥ ♥ ♥

100g buckwheat flour
1 tsp gluten-free baking powder
1 large egg, lightly beaten
250ml almond milk
1 tbsp soya yogurt
1 ripe banana, plus more
   to serve (optional)
organic flavourless oil, to fry
organic maple syrup, to serve
berries, to serve (optional)

Makes 16

In a large bowl, whisk together the flour, baking powder, egg and almond milk until you have a smooth paste. Whisk in 75ml of water and the yogurt to make a smooth batter. Peel and roughly chop the banana and stir it into the batter.

Heat 1 tsp of the oil in a non-stick pan over a medium heat and swirl it around so the base of the pan is completely covered.

Add a few tbsp of the batter to the hot frying pan, leaving a gap between each. Wait until little bubbles start to form on the surface of the pancakes, which should take one or two minutes, then flip. Fry on the other side until golden brown, again about one or two minutes. Wrap the cooked pancakes in a tea towel to keep them warm while you cook the rest.

Serve a stack of the pancakes drizzled with maple syrup, adding banana slices or berries, if you like.

I really, really like porridge. It is just such a useful staple recipe to have at your fingertips on a cold winter's morning. Brown rice is easier to digest than white and so much lighter on my stomach. It keeps me fuller for longer than refined white carbohydrates.

BROWN RICE PORRIDGE

1 vanilla pod
160g cooked Yang brown rice
   (see page 136)
400ml almond milk
pinch of sea salt
2 tbsp dried blueberries
1 tsp ground cinnamon
raw honey, to serve
goji berries, to serve (optional)
grated apple, to serve (optional)
berries, to serve (optional)
bee pollen, to serve (optional)

Serves 2

Split the vanilla pod in half lengthways and scrape out the seeds. Do not discard the vanilla pod, it can be kept for another use.

Place the vanilla seeds, cooked rice, almond milk, sea salt, dried blueberries and cinnamon in a saucepan over a medium heat and bring to a simmer. Let simmer for 20 minutes until the majority of the almond milk has been absorbed.

Serve immediately, drizzled with some honey. Depending on your storecupboard contents or early morning preferences you could add goji berries, grated apple, a handful of berries, or a sprinkling of bee pollen, if you like.

This is a truly satisfying muffin that you can have as a treat for breakfast. One of my friends loves muffins and he never thought they could be healthy. I created this recipe to prove him wrong! They can be good for you and still taste lovely and gooey. Xylitol is a natural sweetener that doesn't cause great spikes in your blood sugar, so it won't make you feel guilty. You can buy it online or at health food shops.

BaNaNa, PeCan& CiNNaMON muFFiNs

300g spelt flour
200g xylitol
pinch of sea salt
2 tsp ground cinnamon
$\frac{1}{2}$ tsp baking powder
$\frac{1}{2}$ tsp bicarbonate of soda
250ml organic flavourless oil
3 eggs, lightly beaten
3 ripe bananas, mashed
100g pecans, chopped

Makes 12

Preheat the oven to 180°C/gas mark 4. Line a 12-hole muffin tray with muffin cases.

Place the spelt flour, xylitol, salt, cinnamon, baking powder and bicarbonate of soda in a large mixing bowl and lightly stir it all together. Place the oil, eggs and bananas into a separate bowl and whisk until combined. Add the wet ingredients to the dry ingredients and lightly stir until just combined. Gently mix in the pecans. Spoon into the muffin cases until each is no more than two-thirds full.

Bake in the oven for 20–25 minutes until risen and golden. When they're ready, a skewer inserted into the middle of a muffin should come out clean. Leave on a wire rack to cool.

ON-THE-GO

snacks&
CHOCOLATES

I get my sweet tooth from my mother (who in turn gets it from her dad) and we have both been fighting a battle with sugar for all of our lives. My mum came up with this recipe and she absolutely adores them. They keep her – and now me, too – going in our moments of need.

almond power balls

330g whole almonds
2 tbsp organic cacao powder
60g dairy-free protein powder
16 medjool dates, pitted
1–2 tsp vanilla extract
1 tsp ground cinnamon
desiccated coconut or chopped
   goji berries, to coat

Makes 14

Place the almonds in a food processor with the cacao and protein powder and blitz until the mixture looks crumbly, but not smooth. Add the dates, vanilla extract and cinnamon and blitz again. Add a splash of water and stir; the mixture should be soft and have come together into a soft ball.

With clean hands, take lumps of the mixture and roll it between your palms to create bite-sized balls. You should end up with about 14 balls.

Fill a large shallow dish with desiccated coconut or chopped goji berries. Roll the power balls in it until completely covered.

Line a container with baking parchment. Place a layer of the power balls in the container and cover with a second sheet of baking parchment, then add another layer of power balls. Repeat until all the balls are boxed. Store in the fridge until needed.

No one wants to miss out on a brownie, especially me. A deliciously sweet brownie just had to go in this book, it wouldn't be complete without it. This recipe is based on an amazing raw brownie I ate in New York, but I have created a not-so-scary version, slightly less raw and far more like the taste and texture we are used to.

maca & macadamia brownies ♥ ♥ ♥

100g macadamia nuts, or walnuts, hazelnuts or pecans
2 pinches of fine sea salt
1 tbsp organic agave syrup
300g medjool dates, pitted
4 tbsp coconut oil, at room temperature
1 tbsp flax seeds
1 tbsp chia seeds
12 tbsp organic cacao powder, plus more to dust
2 tbsp maca powder
$\frac{1}{2}$ tsp vanilla extract
3 of your favourite herbal tea bags (I use Choco Chili by YogiTea), cut open and bags discarded, or 1 tbsp organic ground coffee
handful of flaked almonds, toasted
1 tbsp bee pollen (optional)

Makes 16 slices

Roast the nuts in a dry, hot pan over a medium heat until only just beginning to brown. Add a pinch of salt and the agave syrup and coat all the nuts to let them caramelise lightly. Take the pan off the heat and leave to cool.

In a food processor, blend all the remaining ingredients – apart from the flaked almonds and bee pollen – on a high speed until you have a smooth dough. Don't forget to add another pinch of salt. Scrape the dough on to a piece of baking parchment and knead in the caramelised nuts in by hand. Using your hands or a rolling pin, press the mixture flat to a thickness of about 1.25cm.

Transfer the baking parchment holding the mixture on to a metal or ceramic tray and cover with cling film. Place in the fridge and leave to set for at least 30 minutes.

Dust with cacao powder, cut into about 16 rectangles and sprinkle with the toasted almonds and bee pollen, if using, to serve. Leave out the bee pollen and these brownies become vegan, too.

These are the ideal thing to have in your handbag when you are out and about, or if you know you will be tied up all day. Small yet packed full of flavour and nutrition, they keep you going and perk you right back up when you feel yourself starting to slump...

cranberry &oat energy balls

100g gluten-free oats
50g desiccated coconut
150g raw peanut butter
50g flax seeds
50g dried cranberries
100ml organic maple syrup
1 tbsp chia seeds
1 tsp vanilla extract

Makes 14

Stir all the ingredients together in a large mixing bowl until thoroughly combined. Cover with cling film and place in the refrigerator for at least 30 minutes.

With clean hands, take lumps of the mixture and roll it between your palms to create bite-sized balls. You should end up with about 14 balls.

Line a container with baking parchment. Place a layer of the energy balls in the container and cover with a second sheet of baking parchment, then add another layer of energy balls. Repeat until all the balls are boxed. Store in the fridge until needed.

Make these for when you know you will be dashing about. I get so tempted if I am out when hunger hits, but it's much easier to be good with these in my bag. I carry a couple around and eat them as soon as I feel my sugar levels dropping. As you use gluten-free flour here, adding a little natural xanthan gum stops the bars being too crumbly.

pumpkin seed slice

60g butter
50g xylitol
100ml raw honey
50g of your favourite gluten-free plain flour
$\frac{1}{2}$ tsp xanthan gum
200g pumpkin seeds
100g organic gluten-free muesli

Makes 16 slices

Preheat the oven to 180°C/gas mark 4. Line a baking tray with baking parchment.

Place the butter, xylitol and honey in a saucepan over a low heat and leave until melted.

Put the flour, xanthan gum, pumpkin seeds and muesli in a mixing bowl and add the honey mixture. Stir until well combined. Press the mixture into the lined baking tray in an even layer, then bake for 20–30 minutes until golden.

Leave to cool completely in the tin, then slice into pieces to serve.

These are the ultimate girly treat and so easy to make. They are great to give as gifts as you can give them a personal touch by rolling them in loads of different ingredients, including nuts, coconut or cacao powder. They look wonderful tied up in a pretty bag and have that bitter chocolate hit that many people love. If you have a super-sweet tooth, you can increase the dates and reduce the cacao in this recipe.

CHOCOLATE TRUFFLES

1 tbsp coconut oil, at room temperature
150g medjool dates, pitted
150g macadamia nuts
3 tbsp organic cacao powder
desiccated coconut, organic cacao powder or crushed nuts, to coat

Makes 16

Place the coconut oil, dates, macadamia nuts and cacao powder in a food processor and blitz until you have a rough paste, this will take about a minute.

With clean hands, take bite-sized amounts of the mixture and roll between your palms into little balls. You should end up with about 16 balls.

Fill a large shallow dish with your chosen coating and roll the little truffles in it until completely covered.

Line a container with baking parchment. Place a layer of the truffles in the container and cover with a second sheet of baking parchment, then add another layer of truffles. Repeat until all the truffles are boxed. Store in the fridge until needed.

These are not the most attractive treat, so definitely not one to give as a gift or take to a party, but they are so handy to have in your fridge for when you are craving sugar. They will help keep you from reaching for the digestive biscuits after a good work out...

STICKY DATE BALLS

150g medjool dates, pitted
50g pecan nuts
50g dried apricots
10g organic puffed rice
2 tbsp goji berries
1 tbsp coconut oil, at room
    temperature
pinch of fine sea salt

Makes 12

Place all the ingredients in a food processor and blitz for two minutes or until well combined.

With clean hands, take pieces of the mixture and roll between your palms to form generous-sized balls. You should end up with about 12 balls.

Line a container with baking parchment. Place a layer of the date balls in the container and cover with a second sheet of baking parchment, then add another layer of date balls. Repeat until all the balls are boxed. Store in the fridge until needed.

These are what inspired me to write this book. They were my first encounter with deliciously sweet food that is actually good for you. I was visiting my friend Holly in LA and she had ordered the ingredients to make these. She was very excited about it, but I was less convinced, as I didn't believe they could be good for you *and* delicious. So we made them together. As soon as I tasted them, I was convinced. They are amazing. You should only eat a couple at a time, especially at night, as they can make you slightly over excited! If you can't find mesquite, use an extra 1 tbsp of maca instead.

Mama Holly's Vegan Goji Berry Chocolates ♥ ♥ ♥ ♥

450g cacao butter or coconut oil

300g goji berries, plus more for the top

60ml organic agave syrup, plus more if needed

1 heaped tbsp coconut oil

90g organic cacao powder

1 tbsp maca powder

1 tbsp mesquite powder (optional)

1 tbsp spirulina

Makes 48

Bring a little water to the boil in a saucepan and place a heatproof bowl over it, making sure the water does not touch the bowl. Place the cacao butter in the bowl to melt. Place the goji berries, agave syrup and 110g of the melted cacao butter in a bowl and stir to combine. Leave to soak while you get on with everything else. You can add extra agave and cacao butter if it looks like the berries need more moisture.

To make the chocolate sauce, transfer the rest of the melted cacao butter to a blender and add the coconut oil, cacao powder, maca powder, mesquite powder and spirulina. Blend until completely smooth. Using a funnel, carefully pour the mixture into a squeezy bottle or a jar you can accurately pour from.

Line two 24-hole mini cupcake trays with 48 mini cupcake cases. Carefully pour a layer of the sauce into each, so it just covers the bottom. Place in the freezer to set. Meanwhile, in a food processor, blend the berry mixture until roughly chopped but not smooth.

Once the sauce has set, add ¾ tsp of the berry mixture to each case, then cover with a final layer of sauce and sprinkle with goji berries. Freeze until solid and serve, or store in the fridge until needed.

COOKIES & BISCUITS

A classic American-style chunky cookie with a wonderfully healthy twist. They are so unbelievably easy and quick to make. Recently, my girlfriends Kate and Erin were coming for dinner but were running late. I had 15 minutes to spare so I whipped these up to serve after dinner with coffee. They were more than a little impressed to arrive to a wonderful smell of freshly baked cookies and were extremely pleased to be rewarded for being late!

NUT BUTTER & CHOCOLATE CHIP COOKIES ♥ ♥

250g of your favourite gluten-free plain flour

1 tsp gluten-free baking powder

pinch of fine sea salt

125g organic peanut butter

125g organic hazelnut butter

1 egg, lightly beaten

250g organic maple syrup

5 tbsp organic flavourless oil

1 tsp vanilla extract

100g raw chocolate, broken into small pieces

Makes 16-20

Preheat the oven to 170°C/gas mark 3½. Line one large or two small baking trays with baking parchment.

In a mixing bowl, combine the flour, baking powder and salt and set aside. In another larger bowl, mix together the peanut and hazelnut butters, egg, maple syrup, oil and vanilla extract. Stir until well combined.

Pour the flour mixture into the nut butter mixture, add the pieces of chocolate and stir briefly until only just combined.

Scoop heaped tablespoons of the mixture on to the prepared baking tray(s), leaving a 2cm gap between each as the cookies will spread as they cook. Bake for 10–12 minutes, or until they begin to crack slightly all over. Leave to cool for five minutes on the tray(s), then transfer to a wire rack to cool completely.

I firmly believe my Gramps is the greatest man ever to exist. He always helps his family in any way that he can. To make sure we got our quality time together, he would drive from his house to mine in the morning, then take me to school. So I wanted to try to thank him by including a special recipe just for him. As he adores ginger and has a truly awful sweet tooth, he needs to have a good-for-you recipe too...

Ginger & Hazelnut Biscuits

♥ ♥ ♥ ♥

250g ground almonds

$\frac{1}{2}$ tsp fine sea salt

1 tsp bicarbonate of soda

1 tbsp ground ginger

1 tsp ground cinnamon

$\frac{1}{2}$ tsp vanilla extract

100ml organic flavourless oil

1 tbsp hazelnut oil

60ml organic maple syrup

120ml organic agave nectar

1 tbsp finely grated unwaxed or organic lemon zest

handful of hazelnuts, roughly chopped

Makes 12

Preheat the oven to 180°C/gas mark 4. Line one large or two small baking trays with baking parchment.

In a large mixing bowl, stir together the ground almonds, salt, bicarbonate of soda, ground ginger and cinnamon. In another bowl, combine the vanilla extract, both oils, the maple syrup, agave nectar and lemon zest.

Pour the wet ingredients into the dry ingredients and stir until well combined. Using clean hands, form the mixture into 12 balls and place on the prepared tray(s) about 5cm apart. Slightly flatten each using the palm of your hand. Sprinkle the hazelnuts over the cookies and bake for seven to 10 minutes, until the tops start to crack slightly. Leave to cool for five minutes on the tray(s), then transfer to a wire rack and let cool completely before serving.

A must-have for big chocoholics.
I could eat classic chocolate cookies
by the packet, but these are my much
healthier alternative. Spelt is a denser
flour than plain wheat, so these are
more filling than regular cookies.
I actually feel satisfied after eating only
a couple and don't need to eat all 12 of
them at once...

CHOCOLATE BISCUITS

60g organic oats
180g spelt flour
50g ground almonds
3 tbsp organic cacao powder
75g xylitol
$\frac{1}{2}$ tsp baking powder
pinch of fine sea salt
25ml coconut oil, at room
    temperature
75g coconut butter
60g flaked almonds, toasted

Makes 12

Preheat the oven to 180°C/gas mark 4. Line two baking trays with baking parchment.

Blitz the oats in a food processor until they have taken on a fine breadcrumb-like consistency. Tip them into a large mixing bowl, then stir in the spelt flour, ground almonds, cacao powder, xylitol, baking powder and salt. Mix in the coconut oil, coconut butter and almonds until well combined.

Using your hands, form the mixture into 12 balls and place half on each baking tray, so they are well spread out. Squash the dough balls slightly with the palm of your hand.

Bake for 10–12 minutes or until a lovely golden brown. Leave for five minutes on the tray, then transfer to a wire rack to let cool completely before serving.

I HAVE LEARNED TO

APPRECIATE MY CURVES

Growing up, I absolutely loved lemon slices and would sneakily eat as many packets as I could. I have tried to create a version of that happy taste in these biscuits. The lemon and almond combination is wonderful; the nuts add a lovely depth of flavour and the citrus gives a fabulous freshness.

lemon Biscuits

200g ground almonds
1 tsp gluten-free baking powder
pinch of fine sea salt
4 tbsp coconut oil, at room temperature
2 tbsp organic maple syrup
2 tbsp lemon juice
1 tbsp finely grated organic or unwaxed lemon zest

Makes 12-15

Preheat the oven to 180°C/gas mark 4. Line one large or two small baking trays with baking parchment.

In a large mixing bowl, stir the ground almonds, baking powder and salt. Add the coconut oil, maple syrup, lemon juice and lemon zest and mix until well combined.

Take a tablespoonful of the dough and, using clean hands, roll it into a ball. Place the ball on a prepared baking tray and gently press it down with the palm of your hand to flatten. Continue with the rest of the mixture, leaving enough space in between each cookie on the tray in case they spread as they cook.

Bake for eight to 10 minutes until a lovely golden brown colour. Leave for five minutes on the tray(s), then transfer to a wire rack and let cool for 10–15 minutes before serving.

I love almonds and would eat them in any form in probably any dish! The ground almonds give these biscuits an unbeatable melting quality. And there is a delightful Amaretto flavour to the biscuits, so they are delicious with a warming hot drink.

SPELT & ALMOND BISCUITS

150g spelt flour
50g ground almonds
75g xylitol
$\frac{1}{2}$ tsp baking powder
pinch of fine sea salt
100ml coconut oil, at room temperature
50g flaked almonds, toasted
1 tsp vanilla bean paste

Makes 12

Preheat the oven to 180°C/gas mark 4. Line two baking trays with baking parchment.

In a large mixing bowl, combine the spelt flour, ground almonds, xylitol, baking powder and salt. Stir in the coconut oil, flaked almonds and vanilla bean paste.

Using clean hands, form the mixture into 12 balls and place half on each baking tray. Squash the dough balls slightly with the palm of your hand and position them so that they have room to expand as they cook.

Bake for 10–12 minutes or until golden brown. Leave to cool for five minutes on the trays, then transfer to a wire rack to let cool.

MAKE-YOU-FEEL-GREAT cakes

While researching this book, I went on a babe's holiday to New York with my lovely friend Florence. I was very keen to eat well and she was a great support, helping me to discover new ingredients and trying my concoctions. I promised to create a cake for her, to thank her for keeping me on track. Here is the very orange recipe I came up with for one of my favourite red heads.

Apricot & ginger cake

1 tbsp coconut oil, for the tin

250g ground almonds

$\frac{1}{2}$ tsp sea salt

2 tsp gluten-free baking powder

$1\frac{1}{2}$ tbsp ground ginger

125ml organic agave syrup

3 eggs, lightly beaten

1 tbsp vanilla extract

150g organic dried apricots, quartered

edible petals, to serve (optional)

Serves 8

Preheat the oven to 170°C/gas mark $3\frac{1}{2}$. Gently melt the coconut oil in a small saucepan over a medium heat until just melted. Brush it all over a 20cm cake tin.

In a large mixing bowl, stir together the almonds, salt, baking powder and ginger. In a smaller bowl, mix the agave syrup, eggs and vanilla. Add the wet ingredients to the dry ingredients and mix until just combined, then gently mix in the apricots.

Pour the batter into the prepared tin and bake for 30–40 minutes or until golden brown; a skewer inserted into the centre should come out clean. Leave in the tin for five minutes, then transfer to a wire rack to let cool completely before serving, sprinkled with edible petals, if you like.

This recipe is for my little brother, Alfie. He absolutely adores banana bread and begs my mum to make it whenever she has a spare moment. I bake this really delicious version whenever he comes to stay with me, so he can have it toasted in the morning or as a snack in the afternoon, spread with nut butter, as in the photo here. I think this is so good used as a bread rather than just a cake, especially as it is quite dense due to the rye flour.

Banana Bread

70ml coconut oil
200g rye or spelt flour
50g xylitol
1 tsp baking powder
pinch of sea salt
1 tsp ground cinnamon
3 ripe bananas
4 tbsp soya yogurt
2 eggs, lightly beaten
60ml raw honey
1 tsp vanilla extract

Serves 10

Preheat the oven to 200°C/gas mark 6. Gently melt the coconut oil in a small saucepan over a medium heat until just melted. Brush about 10ml of it all over the inside of a medium loaf tin.

In a large bowl, mix together the flour, xylitol, baking powder, salt and cinnamon. Peel and slice the bananas and place in a separate bowl. Mash the bananas with a fork and stir in the remaining coconut oil, the yogurt, eggs, honey and vanilla. Gently fold the banana mixture into the flour mixture until combined, then pour the batter into the prepared tin.

Bake the bread for about one hour, or until a skewer inserted into the centre comes out clean. If it looks as though it is getting too dark on top as it is baking, cover it with a sheet of foil. Leave in the tin for five minutes, then turn out on to a wire rack to cool.

This recipe is my mum's absolute favourite. It is an unusual and memorable cake, with Moroccan spicing and a ginger twist. It can be served at a dinner party or as a birthday cake, and it is really worth trying to get hold of a selection of edible flowers or rose petals to use on top; fresh flowers make a simple but absolutely stunning decoration.

moroccan orange cake

110ml coconut oil
250g ground almonds
200g xylitol
2 tsp gluten-free baking powder
30g cardamom seeds, plus
   6 split pods
5 eggs
4 tbsp organic agave syrup
3 tsp rose water
finely grated zest and juice of
   2 large organic oranges
2.5cm piece of root ginger
fresh edible flowers, to decorate
   (optional)
coconut milk yogurt, to serve

Serves 8-10

Preheat the oven to 180°C/gas mark 4. Gently melt the coconut oil in a saucepan. Brush about 10ml of it all over the inside of a 20cm springform tin. Set the rest aside to let cool to room temperature.

Stir together the ground almonds, xylitol, baking powder and cardamom seeds in a large bowl. In a separate bowl, whisk the eggs, 1 tbsp of the agave syrup, 2 tsp of the rose water, the orange zest and cooled coconut oil. Pour the wet ingredients into the dry ingredients and mix to combine. Pour the batter into the prepared tin and bake for 35–45 minutes until a skewer inserted in the centre comes out clean. If the top starts to brown before it is cooked, cover with foil for the remaining cooking time.

Peel and finely grate the ginger and, using your hands, squeeze out the juice from the resulting pulp into a bowl. Strain the orange juice into a small saucepan over a medium heat and add the remaining 3 tbsp of agave syrup, 1 tsp of rose water and 6 split cardamom pods. Bring to the boil. Reduce the heat, add 1 tbsp of the ginger juice and simmer for two minutes until syrup-like.

Let the cake cool for five minutes, then pierce all over the top with a skewer and pour the syrup over evenly. Leave the cake to cool and absorb the syrup. Remove from the tin, leaving the split cardamom pods on top. Decorate with edible flowers, if you like. Spoon coconut milk yogurt on each slice before serving.

My dad likes to call this my 'salad cake'. Don't be put off! It has a crunchier texture than regular carrot cake but the spicy flavours are like the original. This is a girly one to enjoy with friends, as it's perfect for when you are trying to be good but are in desperate need of cake! The cashew frosting is genius and can be used to top any other cakes; it tastes wonderfully bad for you. It isn't!

raw carrot cake

For the cake
150g walnuts
150g medjool dates, pitted and chopped
75g organic dried apricots
100g hazelnuts
375g carrots, peeled and grated
1 tbsp each flax and chia seeds
50g desiccated coconut
finely grated zest of 1 orange
pinch of fine sea salt
1 tsp ground cinnamon
$\frac{1}{4}$ tsp ground ginger
pinch of ground nutmeg
100g pumpkin seeds
75g mix of gluten-free oats, brown rice flakes and quinoa flakes, plus more if needed

For the frosting
200g cashew nuts
175ml coconut oil
2 tbsp xylitol, more if needed
1 vanilla pod or 2 tsp extract
1 tbsp lemon juice
pinch of fine sea salt
100g hazelnuts, chopped

Serves 8-10

The night before you make the cake, place the cashews for the frosting in a bowl of water to soak.

Next day, put the walnuts, dates, apricots and hazelnuts in a food processor and blitz until finely chopped. Add the carrots, flax and chia seeds, desiccated coconut, orange zest, salt, spices and 2 tbsp of water and mix thoroughly to form a smooth dough.

Transfer the dough to a work surface and knead in the pumpkin seeds and the oat and flake mixture until you have a good firm dough. Add a little more oat mixture if it is not firm enough. Line a 15–20cm square baking tin with baking parchment. Press the cake mixture into the tin and make the top even.

Make the frosting: gently melt the coconut oil in a small saucepan over a medium heat, then let cool to room temperature. Once cool, whisk with the xylitol until a smooth paste forms. Drain the cashew nuts and place in a food processor. Add 50ml of cold water a little at a time, blitzing after each addition, until a smooth, thick cream has formed. Split the vanilla pod in half lengthways and scrape out the vanilla seeds. Do not discard the pod; this can be used for another purpose. Add the vanilla seeds or extract to the cashew nuts with the lemon juice and sea salt and mix again.

Gradually fold the cashew mixture into the coconut oil mixture until you have a rich, creamy frosting. Check the sweetness and add more xylitol if needed, then use to cover the cake. Refrigerate for at least two hours to ensure the cake sets. To serve, cover with the chopped hazelnuts and cut into generous squares.

This is my winter warmer cake for when it starts to get cold outside. I love to make this for my family and take it back as a present when I go home for Christmas. It has a wonderful depth of flavour and, on a freezing day, a generous slice of this with a cup of tea is my idea of heaven. This is such a treat and I always receive beaming smiles when I arrive in the doorway clutching a tin of this.

APPLE, Cinnamon & HONEY Cake

♥ ♥

210ml coconut oil
350g millet flour, plus more
  to dust
100g xylitol
1 tsp gluten-free baking powder
$\frac{1}{2}$ tsp ground cinnamon
4 eggs, lightly beaten
50g raw honey
2 apples, cored and grated
150g sultanas (optional)

Serves 8

Preheat the oven to 180°C/gas mark 4. Gently melt the coconut oil in a small saucepan over a medium heat until just melted. Brush about 10ml of it all over the inside of a 20cm springform cake tin and line the base with baking parchment. Set the rest of the coconut oil aside to let cool to room temperature.

Place the flour, xylitol, baking powder and cinnamon in a large mixing bowl and stir. In a separate bowl, mix together the eggs, cooled coconut oil, honey and grated apple. Add the egg mixture to the dry ingredients and stir well.

Dust the sultanas, if using, in about 1 tbsp of flour to prevent them sinking to the bottom of the cake. Gently fold them into the batter.

Pour the batter into the prepared tin and bake for 35–45 minutes until the top is golden and a skewer inserted into the centre comes out clean. Leave to cool for 10 minutes in the tin before turning out of the tin, removing the papers and transferring to a wire rack to cool completely.

I WANT WOMEN TO STOP FEELING

GUILTY ABOUT WHAT THEY EAT

This is my more conventional take on carrot cake. The orange adds a wonderful depth of flavour, giving a citrus balance to the sweetness of the carrot. I haven't added any spice, as I really don't think it needs it. This is a great recipe to have up your sleeve, to quickly whip up when you don't have much time to spare.

carrot &orange cake

250g organic butter, at room
   temperature, plus more
   for the tin
150g xylitol
4 eggs, lightly beaten
300g millet flour
1 tsp gluten-free baking powder
2 large carrots, peeled
   and grated
finely grated zest of 2 organic
   oranges
100ml orange juice

Serves 8

Preheat the oven to 180°C/gas mark 4. Butter a 20cm springform cake tin and line the base with baking parchment.

Beat the butter and xylitol for a few minutes until pale and fluffy. Gradually add the eggs, beating well after each addition. Gently fold in the flour and baking powder, then stir in the carrots, orange zest and juice.

Pour the batter into the prepared tin and bake for 45–50 minutes, until the top is golden and a skewer inserted into the centre comes out clean. Leave to cool for 10 minutes in the tin, then turn out of the tin, remove the papers and transfer to a wire rack to cool. Serve in generous slices with a cup of tea.

This is the perfect cake to come home to on a Saturday afternoon after a long, brisk walk. The dates add a sticky gooeyness and the courgettes make the cake exceptionally moist.

courgette &Date cake

150g medjool dates, pitted and
  roughly chopped
150ml organic flavourless oil, plus
  more for the tin
250g of your favourite gluten-free
  plain flour
1 tsp gluten-free baking powder
$\frac{1}{2}$ tsp ground cloves
$\frac{1}{2}$ tsp ground cinnamon
150g palm sugar
60g walnuts, roughly chopped
4 eggs, lightly beaten
2 courgettes, trimmed and grated
  (about 450g)

Serves 8

Place the dates in a heatproof bowl and cover with 50ml of boiling water. Set aside to cool a little.

Preheat the oven to 180°C/gas mark 4. Oil a 20cm springform cake tin and line the base with baking parchment.

Place the flour, baking powder, spices, palm sugar and walnuts in a large bowl. In a separate bowl, beat together the eggs, grated courgettes, remaining oil, dates and their soaking water and mix until well combined. Stir the wet ingredients into the dry ingredients, just until combined.

Pour the batter into the prepared tin and bake in the centre of the oven for 45–50 minutes, until golden on top and a skewer inserted into the centre comes out clean. Leave to cool completely in the tin, then turn out and remove the papers to serve.

SKINNY

PUDDINGS

When you are trying to cut down on unhealthy food, walking past an amazing patisserie or cake shop is *so hard*. The main aim of this book is to make sure you are not deprived of such pleasures, so here is a way to eat a gorgeous thing without having to regret your moment of indulgence afterwards!

summer Berry Tartlets

120g xylitol

handful of mint leaves, roughly chopped

6 blind-baked gluten-free mini tart bases made from Gluten-free tart case (see page 132)

1 quantity Dairy-free creamy custard (see page 128)

300g strawberries, halved or quartered

300g blackberries, halved

200g raspberries

100g blueberries

Serves 6

To make a mint syrup, place 50ml of water and the xylitol in a small saucepan and bring to the boil. Reduce the heat to low and simmer for two minutes until it has a syrup-like consistency. Remove from the heat and cool slightly, then add the mint leaves. Leave to infuse for at least 10 minutes.

Meanwhile, half-fill each of the baked tart cases with the custard. Decorate each tart with a selection of the berries. I like to use the berries to make different patterns on each, to make them look individual. Pour the syrup all over the berries just before serving.

This is almost *too* good. In my opinion, sticky toffee pudding is the ultimate dessert. I was adamant I would create a decadent, gooey, wheat-free sticky toffee pudding that was easily digestible, perfect to follow a Sunday lunch. The is a true success story and makes my mouth water just thinking about it... It is dedicated to one of my favourite Sunday roast buddies, Nick.

STICKY TOFFEE PUDDING ♥ ♥

For the sticky toffee pudding
50g coconut butter, or organic dairy-free margarine, softened, plus more for the tin
175g medjool dates, stoned and roughly chopped
1 tsp bicarbonate of soda
80g coconut palm sugar
80g xylitol
2 eggs, lightly beaten
175g of your favourite gluten-free plain flour
1 tsp gluten-free baking powder
1 tsp xanthan gum
pinch of ground cloves
75g walnuts (optional)

For the sticky toffee sauce
250ml oat cream
150g coconut palm sugar
50g xylitol
100g organic dairy-free margarine

Serves 6–8

Preheat the oven to 180°C/gas mark 4. Use the coconut butter to oil a medium loaf tin, then line the base with baking parchment.

Place the dates, bicarbonate of soda and 300ml of boiling water in a bowl and set aside for 10 minutes to let the dates soften.

Meanwhile, in a large bowl, beat together the remaining coconut butter or spread, the palm sugar and xylitol until well combined. Add the egg a little at a time, beating well after each addition.

Sift the flour, baking powder, xanthan gum and cloves into the butter mixture and gently fold in with a metal spoon. Add the dates and their soaking juices and the walnuts, if using, and fold until everything is just combined.

Pour the batter into the prepared tin and bake for 45–50 minutes or until a skewer inserted in the centre comes out clean.

Meanwhile, make the sauce. Put the ingredients into a saucepan, place over a low heat and let the margarine melt, stirring continuously. Bring to the boil, then reduce the heat to a simmer and cook for 10 minutes, stirring occasionally, until syrupy.

Serve the sticky toffee pudding in slices, with the sticky toffee sauce poured over the top.

I am a firm believer that you should never turn up to a dinner party empty-handed, and bringing a home-made item always goes down far better than anything shop-bought. This is a great dessert to take to a dinner party as you can make it up hours in advance and it can be eaten either hot or cold. The tart looks beautiful and tastes delicious too; a real winner.

Frangipane Tart with Pears

For the frangipane
3 tbsp coconut butter, at
    room temperature
175g ground almonds
3 tbsp organic agave syrup
4 eggs, lightly beaten

For the rest
3 ripe Conference pears
juice of 1 lemon
1 uncooked large tart base made
    from Gluten-free tart case
    (see page 132)
35g pecans, lightly crushed

Serves 8

Preheat the oven to 180°C/gas mark 4.

Place the coconut butter, ground almonds, agave syrup and eggs in a mixing bowl and beat until well combined.

Remove the core from the pears, cut them into roughly equal wedges and place in another bowl. Add a good squeeze of the lemon juice and mix to coat the pears; this will stop them from browning too quickly.

Spread the frangipane over the tart case and lay the pear wedges over the top, following a spiral pattern. Sprinkle the pecans over and bake for 35–40 minutes or until the frangipane is risen, golden and just set. Serve hot, warm or cold.

There is a local crêpe stand I have been going to since I was a very young child and the smell of crêpes cooking makes me so nostalgic. The thought of never being able to eat them because of my wheat intolerance was unbearable, so I am so pleased that I mastered this wonderful recipe.

crêpes suzette

For the crêpes
100g of your favourite gluten-free plain flour
½ tsp xanthan gum
1 tbsp xylitol
pinch of fine sea salt
2 eggs
300ml oat milk
coconut oil, to fry
satsuma segments, to serve (optional)

For the orange sauce
50g coconut oil
5 tbsp xylitol
20g raw honey
150ml freshly squeezed orange juice
finely grated zest of 1 organic orange
finely grated zest of ½ organic or unwaxed lemon
3 tbsp Grand Marnier (optional)

Serves 5

To make the crêpes, sift the flour, xanthan gum, xylitol and salt into a bowl and make a well in the centre. In a smaller bowl, whisk the eggs with the milk, then pour into the well. Whisk the mixture, gradually drawing the flour into the liquid, until well combined with no lumps.

Heat a small crêpe pan or 15cm frying pan over a medium-high heat. Oil very lightly with a little coconut oil, wiping away excess with kitchen paper. Spoon 2 tbsp of the batter into the middle of the pan and immediately tilt and rotate the pan so a thin layer of mixture covers the base. Fry for around 20 seconds, then flip over and cook for a further 30 seconds on the other side until golden spots start to appear. Wrap in a clean tea towel to keep warm while you cook the rest (you should make 15 from this amount), oiling the pan again before adding the batter for each crêpe.

To make the sauce, add the coconut oil, xylitol and honey to a frying pan over a low heat and gently cook until it starts to caramelise. Add the orange juice and zests, increase the heat and cook rapidly for five minutes, or until it thickens. Reduce the heat, add the Grand Marnier, if using, and simmer for two minutes.

To serve, add a crêpe to the frying pan containing the orange sauce and coat well. Fold the crêpe into quarters while it is still in the pan and push gently to the edge. Continue adding the crêpes one by one, coating and folding each as you go. Place three crêpes on each serving plate, drizzle with the remaining sauce and serve with satsuma segments, if you like.

My mum and I discovered this at a friend's house. They challenged us to guess what it was made from and we couldn't believe it when we found it was avocados. We both became completely obsessed with the weird yet wonderful combination of chocolate and avocado. We hunted around for recipes that used it and thought about how we could add different flavours and textures. I have added dates to make it gooey on the base, and banana to take the edge off the avocado. This is just so delicious, I always get lots of requests to make it.

ultimate chocolate & avocado torte

organic dairy-free margarine,
   for the tin
150g desiccated coconut
150g macadamia nuts
$\frac{1}{2}$ tsp ground cinnamon
150g soft, pitted medjool dates
2 avocados
1 banana, peeled
1 tbsp vanilla extract
150g organic cacao powder
120ml organic maple syrup
handful of fresh or dried
   strawberries or raspberries,
   to serve

Serves 12

Use the spread to oil a 20cm springform cake tin, then line the base with baking parchment.

Place the desiccated coconut, macadamia nuts, cinnamon and dates into a food processor. Blitz until the mixture is roughly chopped and well combined. Firmly press into the prepared tin and place in the fridge.

Meanwhile, peel and stone the avocados. In the same food processor as before, combine the avocados, banana, vanilla extract, cacao and maple syrup. Blitz until completely smooth and creamy.

Spoon the avocado mixture over the coconut base and return to the refrigerator for at least two hours, or until firm.

When ready to serve, run a hot knife (dipped in boiling water and then wiped dry) all around the edge of the tin. Carefully remove the torte from the tin, peel off the papers and place on a serving plate. Scatter with fresh or dried berries and serve. Sit back and enjoy the applause.

This is a great finish to a girly dinner as it is really light, refreshing and not too indulgent. The wonderful pink colour is obviously perfectly feminine, too!

ROSÉ POACHED Pears

4 pears
2 vanilla pods
750ml (1 bottle) rosé wine
30g xylitol
100g pistachios
2 tbsp palm sugar
150g mascarpone

Serves 4

Preheat the oven to 180°C/gas mark 4. Line a baking tray with baking parchment.

Peel, core and quarter the pears and slice one of the vanilla pods in half lengthways. Place the pears and split vanilla pod in a saucepan with the wine and xylitol over a high heat. Bring to the boil, then reduce the heat to low and simmer for 20 minutes, or until the pears are tender when pierced with a skewer. Use a slotted spoon to remove them from the pan and place in a bowl to let cool. Increase the heat to medium and let the cooking liquor reduce to a syrupy consistency.

Spread the pistachios out on the prepared baking tray and bake in the oven for 10 minutes.

Meanwhile, place the palm sugar and 2 tbsp of water in a small pan over a medium heat. Cook until all the sugar has dissolved and bubbles start to appear; it should take about five minutes.

Remove the tray of pistachios from the oven and pour the palm sugar caramel over them, ensuring the majority are covered. Leave to set for about 15 minutes, then place in a food processor. Blitz very briefly to create a crunchy praline.

Slice the remaining vanilla pod in half lengthways, scrape out the seeds and mix them into the mascarpone. Do not discard the vanilla pod; this can be used in another dish.

Serve the pears topped with a little rosé syrup, the pistachio praline and the vanilla mascarpone.

I came up with this for my best friend, Joe. He is the one person in the world with whom I can be completely myself, especially when I am in a silly mood. He has been completely obsessed with lemon desserts all his life – lemon curd, lemon biscuits, lemon tarts – he loves them all. This cheesecake is dedicated to his greatness.

Lemon Cheesecake ♥

75g organic butter or coconut oil, melted, plus more for the tin
300g gluten-free biscuits
50g mixed nuts, such as pine nuts and hazelnuts
1 tbsp organic cacao powder (optional)
4 gelatine leaves, or about 4 tsp vegetarian gelatine (check the packet for exact equivalent amounts)
3 egg yolks
65g xylitol
50ml organic double cream, or oat or soya cream
450g organic cream cheese
juice of 1 organic or unwaxed lemon plus the finely grated zest of $1\frac{1}{2}$
blueberries, to serve (optional)

Serves 8

Butter a 20cm springform cake tin and line the base with baking parchment. Place the melted butter, biscuits, mixed nuts and cacao powder, if using, into a food processor and blitz to a breadcrumb-like consistency. Firmly press the mixture into the prepared tin and leave to set in the fridge for at least one hour.

Meanwhile, add the gelatine leaves, if using, to a bowl of cold water and let soak for 10 minutes. Or mix the vegetarian gelatine powder, if using, in just enough boiling water to dissolve. Set aside.

Place the egg yolks and xylitol in a large heatproof bowl over a pan of simmering water, making sure the bowl does not touch the water. Whisk until the xylitol has dissolved, then remove from the heat and leave until just hand hot. Once the gelatine leaves are soft to the touch, remove from the water, squeezing out excess, and add to the egg mixture. Or add the vegetarian gelatine solution to the mixture. Stir well until completely melted. Add the cream and beat until well combined. Stir in the cream cheese, lemon juice and the zest of 1 lemon and beat with a whisk until no lumps remain.

Pour over the biscuit base and refrigerate for at least three hours or until set. Decorate with the remaining lemon zest and some berries, if you like, before serving.

I stumbled across this combination while working on my Ultimate chocolate & avocado torte (see page 88). It is wonderful to be able to enjoy the creaminess of a mousse, just by using avocados to make it healthy. Mousse is such a lovely light dessert and it can be enjoyed after even the heaviest of meals. I really didn't want to miss out on such a treat while trying to be a bit nicer to my body, so I developed this.

Raw chocolate mousse

150g coconut oil
4 ripe avocados
90g organic raw cacao powder
1 tbsp vanilla bean paste
pinch of salt
150g organic agave syrup, plus
   more if needed
raspberries, to serve

Serves 6

Gently melt the coconut oil in a small saucepan over a medium heat until just melted. Let cool.

Peel and stone the avocados. Sift the cacao powder and add it to a food processor with all the other ingredients (except the raspberries). Blitz until completely smooth.

Check the taste and, if it is not sweet enough, add a little more agave syrup. Pour the mixture into six ramekins or pretty small bowls and place in the fridge for two hours until set.

Serve chilled, with a handful of raspberries on the side.

This is just a stunning dessert, if I do say so myself... There is no custard or frangipane so it is a lighter way to enjoy a tart. It is such a simple idea, but looks so impressive. I use figs a lot in season, as they are a wonderfully healthy way to satisfy my sweet tooth. If you fancy being a little more indulgent, layer frangipane (see page 84) under the figs.

FiG Tart WiTH Toasted almonds

1 blind-baked large tart base made from Gluten-free tart case (see page 132)
10 figs
30g flaked almonds
2 tbsp organic maple syrup
soya or coconut milk yogurt, to serve

Serves 8

Preheat the oven to 180°C/gas mark 4.

Quarter the figs lengthways and arrange in the tart case in a pretty concentric pattern, flesh facing upwards. Once you're happy with the design, sprinkle the flaked almonds over the top. Drizzle the maple syrup evenly over the figs.

Cook in the oven for 10 minutes, until the figs are heated through and the almonds are golden. Serve hot, straight from the oven, with yogurt.

I serve these if I am having an outdoor summer party as they look lovely and everyone loves them; especially children... of all ages! Jelly is a seriously light way to enjoy sweet things and it is really easy to make larger batches of these. Use whatever berries you like, I like to use as many different berries as I can as each one will add to the wonderful contrast of sharp and sweet.

summer Berry Jellies
♥ ♥

5 gelatine leaves, or about
    5 tsp vegetarian gelatine
    (check the packet for exact
    equivalent amounts)
750ml organic pure berry juice
50g xylitol
75g strawberries, hulled and
    quartered
200g raspberries
70g redcurrants, stalks
    removed
100g blackberries
60g blueberries

Serves 6

Put the gelatine leaves, if using, in a bowl of cold water and let soak for 10 minutes. Or mix the vegetarian gelatine powder, if using, in just enough boiling water to dissolve. Set aside.

Meanwhile, place the berry juice in a saucepan over a medium heat and bring to a simmer. Stir in the xylitol and cook, stirring all the time, until the xylitol disolves. Remove from the heat and leave until just hand hot.

Once the gelatine leaves are soft to the touch, remove from the water, squeezing out excess, and add to the berry juice mixture. Or add the vegetarian gelatine solution to the mixture. Stir well until completely melted.

Divide a mixture of the berries equally between six glasses. Pour over the berry juice mixture and place in the fridge to set for at least three hours.

Serve straight from the fridge.

This is a truly decadent dessert that will prove hard to resist. Smooth, rich and creamy, your guests will be delighted when you come out of the kitchen carrying this. An easy dish that is a guaranteed crowd-pleaser, you will have people begging you for the recipe.

RICH CHOCOLATE DESSERT ♥

250g organic dark chocolate
2 tbsp organic maple syrup
568ml organic double cream
coconut oil, for the tin
$\frac{1}{2}$ tsp ground cinnamon
handful of dried strawberries,
   to serve

Serves 10

Place the chocolate, maple syrup and 100ml of the cream in a heatproof bowl and place over a pan of barely simmering water; making sure that the bowl does not touch the water. When the chocolate has completely melted, set the bowl aside to cool.

Melt a very little coconut oil and brush it all around the inside of a 22cm springform cake tin. Line the base with baking parchment.

Place the remaining cream and the cinnamon in a large mixing bowl and whip until thick, stiff and glossy. Gently fold in the cooled chocolate mixture, trying not to remove too much of the whipped-in air. Spoon into the prepared tin and leave to set in the fridge for at least three hours, preferably overnight.

Carefully remove from the tin by running a hot slim-bladed knife (dipped in boiling water, then wiped dry) all around the edge and then carefully remove the tin and peel off the papers. Serve chilled, topped with a sprinkling of dried strawberries.

This is a real British staple. Crumble is such a warming, comforting dish that it is perfect for cold, dark winter evenings. The combination of apple and blackberry is a classic, and the pecan crumble topping adds so much flavour to the dish that you will wonder why you ever used anything else.

APPLE, BLACKBERRY & PECAN CRUMBLE

♥

4 cooking apples

1 tsp cornflour

350g blackberries

75g xylitol

100g of your favourite gluten-free plain flour

½ tsp ground cinnamon

100g pecans

50g palm sugar

70g organic butter

1 quantity Dairy-free creamy custard (see page 128) or Vanilla & coconut ice cream (see page 114), to serve

Serves 4

Preheat the oven to 180°C/gas mark 4.

Peel, core and chop the apples into about 1cm cubes. Place in a large, deep ceramic pie dish and toss in the cornflour. Mix in the blackberries, then sprinkle the xylitol over to cover.

Place the flour, cinnamon, pecans, palm sugar and butter in a food processor and blitz until you have a rough breadcrumb texture. Spread the crumble topping over the fruit and press down slightly to ensure that you cannot see any fruit.

Bake the crumble in the oven for 35–40 minutes until the top is golden and the fruit is bubbling at the sides.

Serve immediately with Dairy-free creamy custard or Vanilla & coconut ice cream.

Once you know this recipe, you'll be able to spontaneously decide to make something sweet for dinner guests, without spending too much time away from them. They are a great quick, hot treat. Simple really is often best.

Banana Fritters with cinnamon Dust

♥ ♥

organic flavourless oil, to fry
4 bananas
100g of your favourite gluten-free plain flour
2 tbsp cornflour
80ml ice-cold sparkling water
4 tbsp xylitol
1 tbsp ground cinnamon
Vanilla & coconut ice cream (see page 114), to serve

Serves 4

Fill a deep saucepan with about 5cm depth of oil and place over a medium heat. Make sure the oil comes no more than one-third of the way up the sides of the pan. Be sensible and don't leave the pan unguarded.

Peel and thickly slice the bananas into diagonal wedges. Place the flour and cornflour in a large bowl and gradually whisk in the sparkling water a little at a time. You may not need it all, as you want the batter to be thick. Add the bananas and stir to coat.

Test the oil is hot enough by popping in one of the banana slices; if it bubbles rapidly and starts to fry, it is ready. Once hot enough, deep-fry the banana slices in batches until golden, about three minutes. Carefully remove each cooked slice from the oil with a slotted spoon and place on a sheet of kitchen paper to absorb any excess oil whilst you cook the remaining batches.

In a small mixing bowl, combine the xylitol and cinnamon. Place the fritters on a serving platter or individual plates and sprinkle over the cinnamon dust. Serve hot with a scoop of Vanilla & coconut ice cream.

ice cream

Last time I was in New York, I went to a pop-up restaurant hosted by an amazing couple who are both chefs and musicians. They serve really unusual concoctions, including a melon and cucumber ice cream made with refined sugar and cream. I loved the flavour combination so much that, as soon as I was back in London, I developed a dairy- and refined sugar-free version. This is a superb recipe that has wonderful depth of flavour. Do use a pinch of salt as it makes the ice cream much creamier.

Melon & cucumber icecream
♥ ♥ ♥

1 cantaloupe melon
1 cucumber
4 tbsp raw honey
400ml almond milk, plus more
    if needed
pinch of salt
edible flowers, to serve
    (optional)

Makes about 1 litre

Chop the melon into chunks, removing both the skin and seeds. Chop the cucumber into pieces and place in a blender with the melon and honey. Blend until no lumps remain.

Divide the mixture between two freezable containers and freeze overnight, or for at least eight hours.

Once the mixture has frozen, tip it back into the blender along with the almond milk and salt. Blend until smooth. Taste, and add a little more almond milk if you think it needs to be creamier.

Either cover and keep frozen until needed, or serve immediately, sprinkled with edible flowers, if you like. This ice cream is especially good with Ginger & hazelnut biscuits (see page 54).

A light and elegant way to enjoy an ice. The sharpness from the lemons and limes make this great for enjoying on a hot day. It gives you a nice sweet kick but won't make you feel full, just refreshed. This is a good one to serve if you are feeding someone who is careful about what they eat.

Lemon &Lime Scented Granita

190g xylitol
3 fresh kaffir lime leaves,
   or finely grated zest of
   1 organic lime, plus more
   to serve (optional)
150ml lemon juice
150ml lime juice

Makes about 750ml

Place 450ml of water, the xylitol and lime leaves or zest in a saucepan. Bring to the boil, stirring. Reduce the heat and let simmer for about two minutes, without stirring, until it starts to develop a syrup-like consistency. Set aside to cool for one hour.

Stir the citrus juices into the syrup and pour into a 22cm freezable container. Cover with cling film and freeze for two hours.

Remove from the freezer and use a fork to break up the mixture. Return to the freezer for another hour, then break it up once more. Repeat a final time, or until the mixture is completely crystallised and there is no liquid in the bottom of the container.

To serve, remove the mixture from the freezer five to 10 minutes before it is needed. Scrape the crystals with a fork to break them up and serve scoops of the granita in glasses, topped with lime zest, if you like.

I just had to have a chocolate ice cream recipe in here. I love ice cream as, once it is made, you can keep it in the freezer and bring it out for any moment of need, whether for yourself or for guests. A staple, to keep on hand at all times.

CHOCOLATE & avocado icecream

2 large, ripe avocados
250ml coconut cream
4 tbsp organic maple syrup
6 tbsp organic cacao powder
2 tbsp coconut butter
1 tsp vanilla bean paste

Makes about 500ml

Place all the ingredients into a blender and blitz until completely smooth with no lumps.

Transfer to an ice-cream machine and churn until frozen. Or, if you don't have a machine, put the ice cream in a freezerproof container, place in the freezer and beat well with an electric whisk every hour until the mixture is frozen, about six hours. This is more laborious, but you need to do it to break up any crystals of ice and keep the ice cream smooth.

Cover and keep frozen until needed.

When I was young, my family used to go to a wonderful restaurant near where we lived and, after the meal, we would have coconut ice cream served in a coconut shell. I thought it the most exotic thing in the world. I've recreated the nostalgic dish without dairy. For an extra kick of sweetness, add some of my Coconut caramel sauce (see page 120).

vanilla & coconut icecream

2 x 400ml cans coconut milk
2 vanilla pods, split lengthways
6 egg yolks
140g xylitol

Makes about 1 litre

Place the coconut milk and vanilla pods in a saucepan and bring to the boil over a medium heat. Turn off the heat and leave to infuse for at least 30 minutes.

Place the egg yolks and xylitol in a large heatproof bowl and place over a pan of barely simmering water, making sure the bowl does not touch the water. Whisk the mixture gently until the xylitol has dissolved, the egg yolks are creamy and the whisk leaves a ribbon trail on the surface.

Strain the coconut milk into the thickened egg yolk mixture, setting the vanilla pods aside for another recipe, and carefully stir to combine. Transfer to a clean saucepan, place over a very low heat and stir continuously until the mixture starts to thicken and coats the back of a wooden spoon. Leave to cool completely.

Place the mixture in an ice-cream machine and churn until frozen. Or, if you don't have a machine, put the ice cream in a freezerproof container, place in the freezer and beat well with an electric whisk every hour until the mixture is frozen, about six hours. This is more laborious, but you need to do it to break up any crystals of ice and keep the ice cream smooth.

Cover and keep frozen until needed.

DON'T DEPRIVE YOURSELF OF SUGAR,

JUST EAT THE RIGHT SUGAR

This sorbet is lovely and refreshing and acts as a great palate cleanser at the end of a heavy meal. It delivers a bright hit of flavour without being sickly sweet.

Lemon Sorbet with Lemon Verbena Syrup

♥ ♥ ♥

For the sorbet
finely grated zest and juice of
   2 organic or unwaxed lemons
150g xylitol
75ml fizzy water
1 tbsp glycerine

For the lemon verbena syrup
50g xylitol
small handful of lemon verbena
   or mint leaves, roughly
   chopped, plus more small
   leaves to serve (optional)

Makes about 300g

Place the lemon zest and xylitol in a saucepan, pour in 150ml of regular cold water, place over a high heat and bring to the boil. Reduce the heat to low and let simmer for five minutes. Remove the pan from the heat and stir in the lemon juice, fizzy water and glycerine. Set aside and leave to cool completely.

When the mixture is cool, transfer to an ice-cream machine and churn until frozen. Or, if you don't have a machine, put the ice cream in a freezerproof container, place in the freezer and beat well with an electric whisk every hour until the mixture is frozen, about six hours. This is more laborious, but you need to do it to break up any crystals of ice and keep the sorbet smooth. Cover and keep frozen until needed.

Meanwhile, make the syrup. Place 50ml of water in a saucepan with the xylitol and bring to the boil over a high heat, stirring until the xylitol has dissolved. Reduce the heat and let simmer for five minutes or until syrup-like. Stir in the lemon verbena or mint leaves, remove the pan from the heat and leave to cool completely. Strain out the leaves.

Serve the lemon sorbet in bowls with the syrup drizzled over and a few more leaves sprinkled over the top, if you like.

THE FEMALE FORM IS SO BEAUTIFUL;

AS WOMEN, WE DESERVE TO FEEL

MORE COMFORTABLE IN IT

When I found out last year that I was lactose-intolerant, my first thought was how I would cope without ice cream. I spent a long time coming up with my own versions of ice creams that were easily digestible. I just love this one, it is light and refreshing and so wonderfully good. I get endless requests to make this for when people come round.

Frozen Banana Caramel Ripple

For the frozen banana whip
4 bananas, peeled, plus more
   to serve
150ml chilled Dairy-free creamy
   custard (see page 128)
50ml Coconut caramel sauce
   (see below)

Makes about 300ml

For the coconut caramel sauce
400ml coconut milk
50g coconut palm sugar
2 tbsp coconut butter

Makes about 400ml

Line a baking sheet with baking parchment. Chop the bananas into 2.5cm rounds and place on the baking sheet, leaving a gap of at least 1cm between each. Place in the freezer for 1½ hours or until the banana slices are frozen.

Meanwhile, make the caramel sauce: place all the ingredients in a small saucepan over a high heat and bring to the boil, stirring occasionally. Boil rapidly for about five minutes. Leave to cool and store in a sealed container in the fridge until ready for use. This can be served hot or cold.

Transfer the frozen bananas and chilled custard to a food processor and blitz until smooth with no lumps left. Place the mixture in a freezable container and drizzle over the coconut caramel sauce. Briefly and gently fold it in to create a ripple effect.

If the mixture has become too liquid, cover and freeze for about 30 minutes to firm up, otherwise this can be served immediately, with banana slices. Any leftovers can be kept in the freezer for future use.

BARE

ESSENTiALS

Being an absolute sugar addict, I am completely obsessed by hot chocolate. I could drink it endlessly, especially in the colder months. When I found out I was lactose-intolerant, I was fearful of losing out on one of my favourite treats. Thankfully, my wonderful friend Jonah saved me from such misery by giving me this dairy-free recipe. Trust me, you will have absolutely no idea that it is made with alternative ingredients and it is truly addictive. It is also low in calories compared to most hot chocolate, which is good as I could drink mugs and mugs of it...

JONAH'S INDULGENT HOT CHOCOLATE
♥ ♥ ♥

240ml Almond & vanilla milk (see page 136), or simply almond milk
1 tsp organic cacao powder
2 tsp xylitol

Serves 1

Heat the Almond & vanilla milk or almond milk in a small saucepan over a medium heat – or in the microwave – until hot but not boiling. In your favourite mug, mix together the cacao and xylitol until evenly mixed with no lumps.

Once the milk is hot and starting to form a slight foam, add a splash of it to the cacao mixture and whisk with a small whisk or fork to form a smooth paste. Gradually stir in more and more of the hot milk... and voila! Low calorie, yummy hot chocolate.

If you find that you have a bit of time in the morning and want something extra-sweet, make a batch of these to serve over your porridge. Or you can use the apricots to make your own version of a gluten-free tart, just fill a Gluten-free tart case with Dairy-free creamy custard or Frangipane (see pages 132, 128 and 84) before arranging the apricots on top.

vanilla poached apricots

12 ripe apricots
2 vanilla pods or 1 tsp vanilla
   bean paste
4 tbsp xylitol

Serves 2

Halve the apricots and remove and discard the stones. Split the vanilla pods lengthways, if using. Place 250ml of water, the vanilla pods or paste and xylitol in a shallow saucepan and bring to the boil over a medium heat. Add the apricots and reduce the heat to a very low simmer. Leave to poach for 10 minutes.

Using a slotted spoon, remove the apricots from the liquid and place in serving dishes. Increase the heat under the poaching liquid to high. Once it is at a rapid boil, leave for five minutes to reduce to a syrup.

Serve warm or cold, drizzled with a little of the syrup. For an extra special treat, serve with ice cream and finely grated organic or unwaxed lemon zest.

This is always a winner. I love it on my Rosé poached pears, Sticky toffee pudding or inside a Gluten-free tart case with some fruit piled on top (see pages 90, 82 and 132). This is a useful recipe to have as it's good to pour over your dessert after a Sunday roast or dinner party.

Dairy-Free Creamy Custard

250ml organic rice milk
2 egg yolks
2 tbsp xylitol
1 tbsp cornflour
$\frac{1}{2}$ tsp vanilla bean paste

Makes about 300ml

Place the rice milk in a saucepan over a medium heat and bring to the boil. Once it reaches the boil, remove from the heat.

In a separate saucepan, but off the heat, whisk together the egg yolks, xylitol, cornflour and vanilla bean paste until there are no lumps remaining. Gradually whisk in the hot rice milk and place the saucepan over a low heat.

Bring the mixture to a very gentle simmer, stirring constantly. The custard should have a thick, glossy texture; this will take about five minutes.

Serve hot, poured over your favourite pudding, or chill and use to fill a tart case (if you chill it, whisk it for a final time before using, to ensure the custard is beautifully smooth).

I love the contrasting textures here, from the smooth, indulgent porridge and crunchy granola to the fresh, bright fruits. A great thing about this porridge is that you can mix and match according to what you fancy; you can have carbs from the brown rice or protein from the quinoa, or you can even have both. Whatever you choose, you can be safe in the knowledge that it will be good for you!

Life is Sweet Blueberry Porridge

100g cooked Yang brown rice or
   cooked Quinoa (see pages
   133 and 136), or both
240ml organic rice milk, plus
   more if needed
1 tbsp coconut oil
50g Rise & shine granola
   (see page 14)
small handful of blueberries or
   other fruit of your choice
almond milk, to serve

Serves 2

Place the cooked rice or quinoa or a mixture of both in a small saucepan with the rice milk and place it over a high heat. Just as it reaches the boil, reduce the heat to low and leave to simmer for 10 minutes, stirring every so often to prevent it from sticking to the pan. The grains should absorb the milk and become soft. If it is too dry, just add a little more rice milk, being careful not to add too much as that will make it watery.

Once it has reached a soft-but-not-wet consistency, stir in the coconut oil and let it simmer for a further three minutes.

Divide the mixture between two bowls and top each with the granola and blueberries. Sprinkle on a little almond milk to serve.

Utterly delicious added to porridge. The banana gives a lovely sweetness and the nuts a wonderful texture. This is the sort of recipe that allows you to sprinkle your own creative flair over dishes that you eat every day.

caraMELiSED Bananas WiTHcrunCHY almonDs

♥ ♥ ♥ ♥

4 bananas
2 tbsp coconut oil
2 tbsp palm sugar
100g flaked almonds

Serves 4

Peel the bananas and cut them into wedges, as in the photo. Place a large frying pan over a medium heat. Add the coconut oil and heat gently, swirling the pan to make sure the base is covered with the oil. Add the palm sugar and, without stirring, cook until the sugar is dissolved and just slightly bubbling, this should take about three minutes. Using a wooden spoon, stir in the bananas and cook until they are soft and golden, six to 10 minutes.

Place the almonds in a dry frying pan and place over a medium-high heat. Toss them for about four minutes, or until golden, shaking the pan to prevent them from burning.

Serve the bananas with the almonds sprinkled over the top, or with porridge, quinoa, coconut milk yogurt or dairy-free ice cream.

As this tart case lacks gluten, inevitably the pastry is on the crumbly side and needs to be handled with care. It will be a little tricky to roll and does have a tendency to break up as it is transferred to the tin. Just make sure you patch up any holes and it will be fine.

GLUTEN-FreeTart case

125g organic soya spread, plus more for the tin(s)

250g of your favourite gluten-free plain flour

1 tsp xanthan gum

1 tbsp xylitol

1 egg, lightly beaten

pinch of fine sea salt

Makes enough for 1 large (22cm) tart or 6 mini (8cm) tartlets

Use the soya spread to oil generously a 22cm loose-bottomed tart tin or six 8cm tartlet tins.

Place the flour, soya spread, xanthan gum, xylitol, egg and salt in a food processor. Blitz for about 30 seconds until the mixture starts to come together and form a dough. Pull the mixture into a ball, wrap in cling film and refrigerate for at least 45 minutes.

Roll out the dough between two sheets of cling film until it is big enough to fit the tart tin(s) and about 5mm thick.

Peel off the cling film and transfer the rolled-out dough to the tart tin(s). The pastry may break up a little at this stage; don't worry, this is normal, you will be able to press it back together once it is in the tin(s). Firmly press the dough into the tin(s), trim any excess from the top edges and use the scraps of dough to patch up broken areas. Place the cases in the fridge for another 20 minutes. Preheat the oven to 180°C/gas mark 4.

Line the pastry with baking parchment and fill with baking beans. Blind-bake the tarts, baking the large tart for 20 minutes or the mini tartlets for 12 minutes, until golden. Remove from the oven, remove the baking beans and parchment and leave to cool in the tin. See pages 81, 84 and 99 for my favourite ideas on what to put in your tarts!

If you are looking for a wonderful, nutritious option then quinoa is perfect. It is full of protein, vitamins and minerals, is very low in fat, great to eat after exercise and for supporting a vegetarian diet. This basic recipe can be used to make Life is sweet blueberry porridge (see page 129), or try a little in some of my power balls (see the On-the-go snacks & chocolates chapter), or you can even add it to a fruit salad!

175g mixed quinoa, such as white, red and black

pinch of fine sea salt

Makes about 200g

It is vital to wash quinoa very thoroughly before use, as it can be gritty and may taste bitter otherwise. Place the grains in a large bowl and fill with cold water under a fast-running tap while mixing with your fingers to clean. Drain in a fine-mesh sieve and repeat at least three times, or until the water runs clear. Leave to drain a final time for a few minutes before cooking.

Place the quinoa, salt and 500ml of water in a saucepan over a high heat and cover with a lid. Once the water comes to the boil, reduce the heat to low and let it simmer. Cook for 15 minutes until all the liquid has been absorbed. The grains should be moist and separated. If all the water has been absorbed but the quinoa is still a little hard, add a small amount more water and take the pan off the heat. The quinoa will continue to soak up the moisture.

Now you can either use the quinoa straight away as a side dish, or let it cool, transfer it to a container and keep in the fridge ready to make porridge for breakfast!

This is a true symphony of flavours; from the sweet strawberries and fragrant thyme, to the twist of orange and hit of pomegranate. You can make this with different berries, and add even more variety by using other herbs such as rosemary and lavender.

strawberry & pomegranate compote

♥ ♥ ♥

2 pomegranates
1kg strawberries, hulled
250g raspberries
100g xylitol
finely grated zest of 1 large
    organic orange plus 1 tbsp
    orange juice
bunch of lemon thyme, tied
    together by the stalks with
    kitchen string

Makes about 1 litre

Cut the pomegranates in half. Using a wooden spoon, hit the uncut side of the pomegranate halves over a mixing bowl so that the seeds are released and fall into the bowl. Discard the peel and white membrane. Place the strawberries, raspberries and pomegranate seeds, 240ml of water and the xylitol in a heavy-based saucepan over a medium heat. Gently crush the fruit with a fork or spoon to break it up slightly and release all the juices. Let it all come to the boil, stirring occasionally.

Once it comes to the boil, reduce the heat, add the orange zest and suspend the bunch of thyme in the bubbling mixture by tying the end of the string to the saucepan handle. Leave to simmer very gently, uncovered, for about one hour, or until most of the water has evaporated and the fruit mixture has a rich, sticky consistency. Stir occasionally and check it is not catching on the pan.

Meanwhile, put some Kilner jars through a hot, quick cycle of the dishwasher. Leave them in there once the cycle has finished.

Add the orange juice to the compote and leave to simmer for five minutes, then remove and discard the bunch of thyme.

Transfer the mixture to the sterile jars while it and the jars are still warm. Tightly secure the lids and place the jars upside down to form a vacuum. Leave at room temperature until cool and slightly set. You can use this like jam on toast, or add a dollop to your morning porridge. Keep refrigerated after opening.

ALMOND & VANILLA MILK

♥ ♥ ♥ ♥

Although you can buy almond milk in cartons, it is well worth making your own. This is the one ingredient that I use more than anything else, in tea, cakes, cookies, ice cream and on cereal. It is extremely good for you, easy to digest and tastes delicious. It is just so useful; you will find you need this made up for all occasions.

175g raw almonds
2 vanilla pods

Makes about 750ml

The night before, place the almonds in a bowl and add enough cold water to cover. Leave to soak overnight.

In the morning, drain the almonds. Cut the vanilla pods in half lengthways and scrape out the seeds. Do not discard the empty pods; they can be kept for a variety of uses. Place the drained almonds, 720ml of fresh cold water and the vanilla seeds in a blender and blitz until smooth. Strain the liquid through a muslin cloth or a very fine sieve into an airtight container.

Store in the fridge for up to three days.

YANG BROWN RICE

♥ ♥ ♥ ♥

Short-grain brown rice is one of the most-used grains in macrobiotic cooking. The macrobiotic philosophy is to balance the yin and yang energies in our bodies through food and, as brown rice is mildly yang, it is considered to be very grounding. Plus it helps to clean your body and eliminate toxins; a good start to any day!

250g short-grain brown rice
good pinch of fine sea salt

Makes about 400g

Using a colander, rinse the rice at least three times and drain thoroughly. Place the rice, 850ml of water and the salt in a saucepan over a low heat, cover and slowly bring to the boil.

Reduce the heat and simmer for 40–50 minutes, stirring once or twice to stop it sticking to the pan. Make sure you replace the lid quickly after each stir to avoid losing too much steam. The rice should absorb all the water and have a lovely firm and slightly chewy grain.

Keep in an airtight container in the fridge for up to two days (no more) until needed. If it gets a bit starchy, rinse it under cold water before using.

index

PROP CREDITS

Anthropologie

www.bimblot.com; quirky French
finds

The Conran Shop

The Linen Works;
www.thelinenworks.co.uk

Samantha Frankel Ceramics
samanthafrankel@me.com; hand-
made lace-embossed and gold-
edged ceramics

THankYOUs

Firstly I would like to thank my extraordinarily wonderful mum for encouraging me to create this book. Without her, my love of baking, my love of the female form and my quest for healthy treats would have never been so passionate! I love you more than anyone else in the world. To my dearest DannyDad, I am so grateful for all of your cooking wisdom, your honesty and your loving support always. My dearest siblings Alfie, Frankie and Betty, thank you for bringing joy to every day of my life. A huge thank you goes to my grams Lee and my gramps Eddie for your unconditional love. To my godmother Zoe Grace, thank you for being a constant source of wisdom and light. You are a complete goddess. Thank you to Eleanor Harrison from Sage and Honey for inspiring me to write this book with your incredible creations, your food really does love the body from the inside, out. Dearest Gavin, my wonderful dad, thank you for teaching me how inventive I can be in the kitchen, your brain and your heart always astound me. Thank you my darling angel bunny Joseph Reuben for being my guinea pig while recipe testing and always putting the biggest smile on my face. To Jonah Pontzer for teaching me something new every day with that big beautiful heart of yours. To my baking partner Martha Freud and the greatest bubba Nancy because thanks to you both, the creative limits of my baking have been stretched further than I could have ever wished.

Thank you to the angel that is Gabriele Luppi. Your cooking enlightened me to a whole new world of flavour and health. You're an absolute hero. To my darling wifelet Florence, I love learning how to be better to my body with you. Donna Rooney and Harry Sprout at Black Book Co-Op, I am so incredibly grateful to you two for making me

feel held, so I have felt comfortable to express myself creatively, and for generally being absolute geniuses, my two wonder women. Thanks to the Blair partnership and everyone at Quadrille for believing in me and making this book actually exist! Thank you to the beautiful Naomi Shimada, for your powerful love of the female form. To Kate Moross for being a true friend, visionary and ultimate supporter of female empowerment. To my dearest mama Holly Miranda for inspiring me to write this whole book, and teaching me that healthy can be delicious. You are a true visionary and such an important part of my soul family.

To my mentor Yvonne Williams, words cannot express how grateful I am to you for your loving power which has helped me to grow and empowered me to create this. To my dearest bird, Katie Williams, thank you for allowing me to educate you about a healthier way to look after that gorgeous body of yours. Thank you Simon Jones and Hackford Jones for taking such good care of me. Beautiful Maire, thank you for your enlightening me to be a much better woman. Thank you to the dearest Kate Halfpenny, your love is one in a million.

And thank you Miss Portia Freeman for being the salt to my pepper, you have one of the kindest souls I've ever known. Thanks to Russell Bateman for making me look after my body in a way I never knew was possible. And the biggest thank you goes to every person who has picked up this book. I hope that it makes you feel good about the body you are lucky enough to live in, and that it helps you to love yourself from your core to every inch of your skin. I love you all with all my heart.

Daisy x

Editorial director *Anne Furniss*
Creative director *Helen Lewis*
Portraits *Guy Aroch*
Food photography *Ali Allen*
Food photographer's assistant
    Rebecca Jane Callaby
Designer *Gemma Hogan*
Editors *Louise McKeever &*
    Lucy Bannell
Endpaper photography *Steve McCabe*
Fashion stylist *Celestine Cooney*
Make-up artist *Florrie White*
Hair stylist *Lyndell Mansfield*
Tester and food stylist *Emily Jonzen*
Tester and food stylist's assistants
    Matthew Ford & Natalie Thomson
Production controller *Sarah Neesam*
Production director *Vincent Smith*

First published in 2014 by
Quadrille Publishing Limited
Alhambra House
27–31 Charing Cross Road
London WC2H 0LS
www.quadrille.co.uk
Text © 2014 Daisy Lowe
Photography © 2014 Guy Aroch &
    Ali Allen
Design and layout © 2014
    Quadrille Publishing Limited

ISBN 978 184949 375 8

Printed in China